Pet Sitting Business Book:

How to Start & Finance a Pet Sitter, & Pet Daycare Home-Based Business

by
Brian Mahoney

Join Our VIP Mailing List and Get FREE Money Making Training Videos! Then Start Making Money within 24 hours!
Plus if you join our Mailing list you can get Revised and New Edition versions of your book free!

And Notifications of other FREE Offers!

Just Hit/Type in the Link Below

https://mahoneyproducts.wixsite.com/win1

Get Massive Money for Real Estate Now!

1. Private Lending and Hard Money (Text Manual) (similar guides have sold for $1,500.00 alone)

2. Real Estate Investing Guide (Text Guide)

3. Goldmine Government Grants (Video Training Program)

4. Residential Government Grant Programs (Video Training Program)

5. Commercial Government Grant Programs (Video Training Program)

6. Creative Financing (Video Training Program)

7. Expert Credit Repair (Video Training Program)

8. Million Dollar Video Marketing (Video Training Program)

9. Customer List Building (Video Training Program)

10. Massive Web Site Traffic (Video Training Program)

11. SEO Marketing (Video Training Program)

12. Bonus 1000 Package!!!

Just Hit the Link Below Right Now!!!

Don't Wait....You'll Wait Your Life Away...

http://www.BrianSMahoney.com

Table of Contents

Chapter 1 — Pet Sitter Business Overview

Chapter 2 — Step by Step

Chapter 3 — Business Plan

Chapter 4 — Business Funding

Chapter 5 — Business Grants

Chapter 6 — Customer Service

Chapert 7 — Zero Cost Marketing

Chapter 8 — Wholesale Business Supplies

Chapter 9 — Business Rolodex

Chapter 10 — Business Terms

ABOUT THE AUTHOR

Brian Mahoney is the author of over 425 business start-up guides, real estate investing programs and Christian literature. He started his company MahoneyProducts in 1992.

He served in the US Army and worked over a decade for the US Postal Service. An active real estate investor, he has also served as a minister for the Churches of Christ in Virginia and Michigan.

He has degree's in Business Administration and Applied Science & Computer Programming.

His books and video training programs have helped thousands of people all over the world start there own successful business.

http://www.briansmahoney.com/

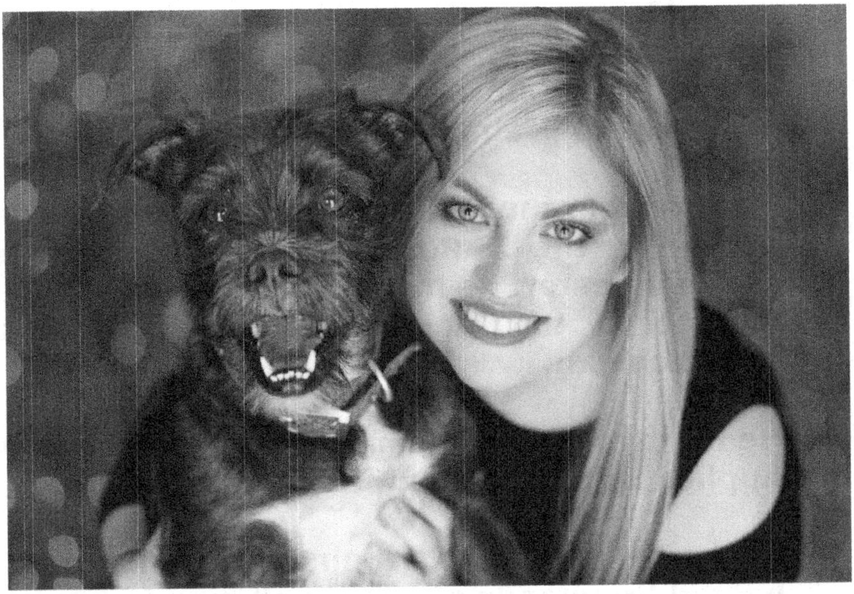

Chapter 1

Pet Sitter Business Overview

Pet Sitter

Business Overview

Start-up Cost:

$150-$200

Advertising:

Word of mouth, Flyers in Vets office & Pet supply stores, Zero Cost Online Marketing, Internet Marketing, Business Cards, Classified Ads, Yellow Pages, Online Yellow Pages, Website, Referrals, Direct Mail Postcards, Business Groups

Equipment Needed:

Vehicle, Pet sitting software, Phone, computer, fax/printer, e-mail, hammer and nails for posting signs.

Hidden Costs:

Insurance & licensing; Travel Expenses, Trip to Vet

Pet Sitter

Business Overview

Home Business Potential:

Yes

Potential Earnings:

$10,000-$25,00

Typical Fees:

$25 per day for one pet $5 for each additional pet. Additional for walking, house training for puppies, holidays or special medical care.

Qualifications:

Love of Animals, Animal 1st Aid, Organization skills

Staff Required:

No (yes for a backup)

Pet Sitter

Business Overview

Pet Sitting

A pet sitter takes care of a pet, usually at the pet owners residence, although sometimes a pet is dropped off at the pet sitter's place of business.

A pet sitter should have a great love for animals, be patience, and have a basic understanding or animal care and first aid.

Pet Sitters International says that it's members had close to 20 million jobs and saw revenue close to 400 million dollars.

Pet sitters give their clients several advantages over regular pet care choices.

* Their pet is more comfortable because it gets to stay in it's home

* Their pet is not exposed to sickness from other pets.

Pet Sitter

Business Overview

* Pet sitters would have less requirements than a kennel.

* Some pet sitters will exercise and clean pets.

There are more households with pets than have children, so many new pet sitting businesses are being started.

Pet sitters usually offer vacation care and dog walking.

Vacation care

Vacation care is usually the main reason for having a pet sitter. A pet sitter visits the client's home for about 30 minutes to admister several duties:

Pet Sitter

Business Overview

* Feeding the pet

* Exercise the pet

* Give the pet medication & vitamins

* Keep an eye on the health of the pet

* Arrange for medical treatment if the pet gets ill

Pet owners are usually billed on a per-vist or per-day basis. A client may also be charged extra for multiple pets, travel expenses and house sitting.

Dog walking

Pet sitters will usually offer dog walking services. In addition, a pet sitter my offer jogging, running, and dog scootering.

Some areas require professional dog walkers to be licensed and have their vehicle inspected for dog transportation.

Pet Sitter

Business Overview

Additional services

Some pet sitters may also offer additional pet services, such as:

* dog boarding

* dog grooming

* a trip to the vet.

These other services may require a license or additional regulation.

Insurance

Commercial or professional pet sitters usually have business insurance. Pet sitter insurance usually covers pet transportation and liability. Petcareins.com insurance policies currently start at $129 a year.

Pet Sitter

Business Overview

General Liability

This coverage will help you with the cost of claims that you become legally responsible for due to injury or damages sustained by a third party during the course of your business operations.

Animal Bailee Coverage

This provides your pet business with coverage should you become legally liable for injuries or damages sustained by an animal in your care, custody, or control.

Vet Bill Reimbursement

This provides coverage for medical expenses—regardless of who is at fault—for a client's pet in your care, custody, or control.

Pet Sitter

Business Overview

Lost Key Liability Coverage

If you were to lose the keys to a client's residence, this coverage could help you manage the cost of installing new locks or having the building rekeyed.

Certification for Professional Pet Sitters

Organizations like Pet Sitters International offer training and testing for professional pet sitters credentialization and accreditation.

Pet Sitter

Business Overview

Other certification may require:

* A criminal background check

* Proof of Insurance

* Require Bonding

* Pet First Aid certification

* Other business documentation

Several businesses including the Red Cross, offer training in first aid.

Summary

Pet Sitting is a growing business and has a low entry barrier. If you love animals and get the proper training and certification, then this business could give you joy, end money worries and give you peace of mind.

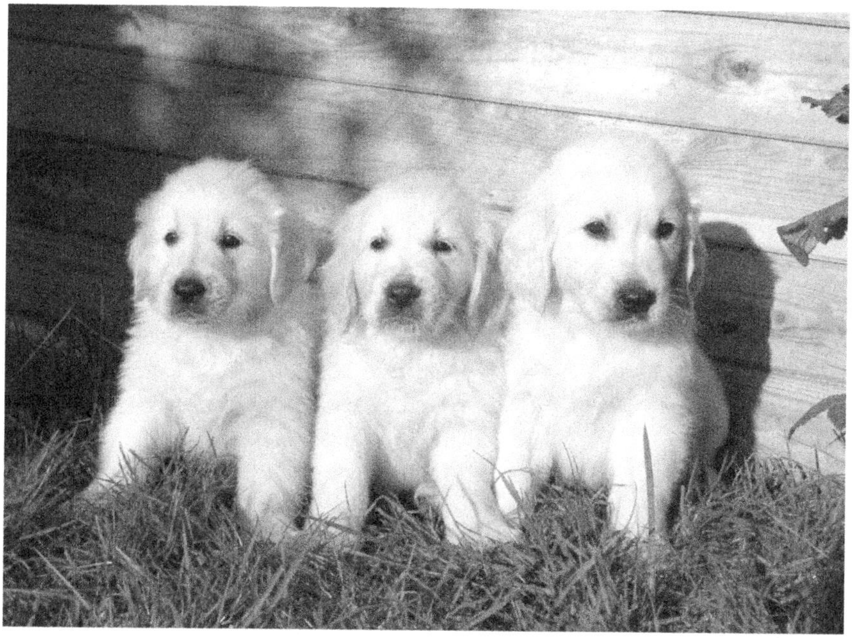

Chapter 2

Getting Started in Business Step by Step

Getting Started in Business

There are over thirty million home-based businesses in the United States alone.

Many people dream of the independence and financial reward of having a home business. Unfortunately they let analysis paralysis stop them from taking action. This chapter is designed to give you a road map to get started. The most difficult step in any journey is the first step.

Anthony Robbins created a program called Personal Power. I studied the program a long time ago, and today I would summarize it, by saying you must figure out a way to motivate yourself to take massive action without fear of failure. Usually that way is giving yourself powerful whys.

2 Timothy 1:7 King James Version

"For God hath not given us the spirit of fear; but of power, and of love, and of a sound mind."

Getting Started in Business

STEP #1 MAKE AN OFFICE IN YOUR HOUSE

If you are serious about making money, then redo the man cave or the woman's cave and make a place for you to do business, uninterupted.

STEP #2 BUDGET OUT TIME FOR YOU BUSINESS

If you already have a job, or if you have children, then they can take up a great deal of your time. Not to mention well meaning friends who use the phone to become time theives. Budget time for your business and stick to it.

STEP #3 DECIDE ON THE TYPE OF BUSINESS

You don't have to be rigid, but begin with the end in mine. You can become more flexible as you gain experience.

Getting Started in Business

STEP #4 LEGAL FORM FOR YOUR BUSINESS

The three basic legal forms are sole proprietorship, partnership, and corporation. Each one has it's advantages.

Go to

https://www.sba.gov/business-guide/launch-your-business/choose-business-structure

https://goo.gl/LJMWNK

and learn about each and make a decision.

STEP #5 PICK A BUSINESS NAME AND REGISTER IT

One of the safest ways to pick a business name is to use your own name. Your own name is not copywrited.

However, always check with an Attorney or the proper legal authority when dealing with legal matters.

Getting Started in Business

STEP #6 WRITE A BUSINESS PLAN

This would seem like a no brainer. No matter what you are trying to accomplish you should have a blueprint. You should have a business plan. In the NFL about seven headcoaches get fired every season. So in a very competetive business, a man with no head coaching experience got hired by the NFL's Philadelphia Eagles. His name was Andy Reid. Andy Reid would later become one of the most successful coaches in the team's history. One of the reasons the owner Jeffrey Lurie hired him, was because he had a business plan the size of a telephone book. Your business plan does not need to be nearly that big, but if you plan for as many things as possible, you are less likely to get rattled when things don't go as planned.

STEP #7 PROPER LICENSES & PERMITS

Go to city hall and find out what you need to do, to start a home business.

Getting Started in Business

STEP #8 SELECT BUSINESS CARDS, STATIONERY, BROCHURES

This is one of the least expensive ways to not only start your business but to promote and network your business.

STEP #9 OPEN A BUSINESS CHECKING ACCOUNT

Having a separate business account makes it much easier to keep track of profit and expenses. This will come in very handy, whether you decide to do your own taxes or hire out an professional.

STEP #10 TAKE SOME SORT OF ACTION TODAY!

This is not meant to be a comprehensive plan to start a business. It is meant to point you in the right direction to get started. You can go to the Small Business Administration for many free resources for starting your business. They even have a program(SCORE) that will give you access to many retired professionals who will advise you for free!

www.score.org

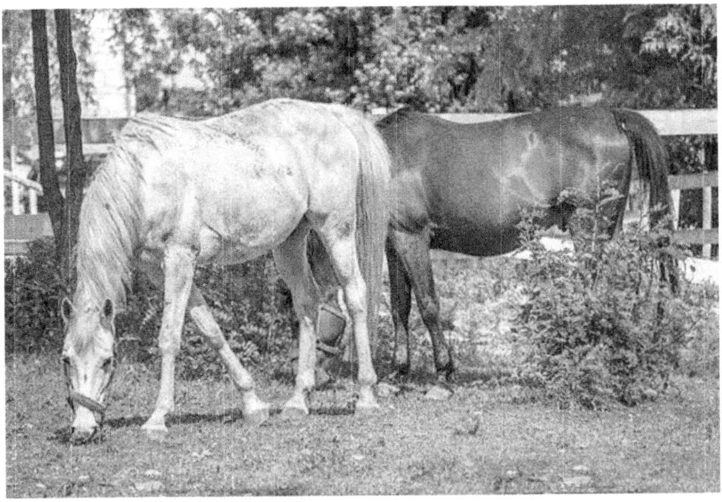

Chapter 3

Writing a Business Plan

How to Write a Business Plan

Millions of people want to know what is the secret to making money. Most have come to the conclusion that it is to start a business. So how to start a business? The first thing you do to start is business is to create a business plan.

A business plan is a formal statement of a set of business goals, the reasons they are believed attainable, and the plan for reaching those goals. It may also contain background information about the organization or team attempting to reach those goals.

A professional business plan consists of eight parts.

1. Executive Summary

The executive summary is a very important part of your business plan. Many consider it the most important because it this part of your plan gives a summary of the current state of your business, where you want to take it and why the business plan you have made will be a success. When requesting funds to start your business, the executive summary is an chance to get the attention of a possible investor.

How to Write a Business Plan

2. Company Description

The company description part of your business plan gives a high level review of the different aspects of your business. This is like putting your elevator pitch into a brief summary that can help readers and possible investors quickly grasp the goal of your business and what will make it stand out, or what unique need it will fill.

3. Market Analysis

The market analysis part of your business plan should go into detail about your industries market and monetary potential. You should demonstrate detailed research with logical strategies for market penetration. Will you use low prices or high quality to penetrate the market?

4. Organization and Management

The Organization and Management section follows the Market Analysis. This part of the business plan will have your companies organizational structure, the type of business structure of incorporation, the ownership, management team and the qualifications of everyone holding these positions including the board of directors if necessary.

How to Write a Business Plan

5. Service or Product Line

The Service or Product Line part of your business plan gives you a chance to describe your service or product. Focus on the benefits to the customers more than what the product or service does. For example, a air conditioner makes cold air. The benefit of the product is it cools down and makes customers more comfortable whether they are driving in bumper to bumper traffic or a sick and sitting in a nursing home. Air Conditioners fill a need that could mean the difference between life and death. Use this section to state what are the most important benefits of your product or service and what need it fills.

6. Marketing and Sales

Having a proven marketing plan is essential element to the success of any business. Today online sales are dominating the marketplace. Present a strong internet marketing plan as well as social media plan. YouTube videos, Facebook Ads and Press Releases all can be part of your internet marketing plan. Passing out flyers and business cards are still an effective way to reach potential customers.

Use this part of your business plan to state your projected sales and how you came to that number. Do your research on similar companies for possible statistics on sales numbers.

How to Write a Business Plan

7. Funding Request

When you write your Funding Request section of your business plan, be sure to be detailed and have documentation of the cost of supplies, building space, transportation, overhead and promotion of your business.

8. Financial Projections

The following is a list of the important financial statements to include in your business plan packet.

Historical Financial Data

Your historical financial data would be bank statements, balance sheets and possible collateral for your loan.

Prospective Financial Data

The prospective financial data section of your business plan should show you potential growth within your industry, projecting out for at least the next five years.

You can have monthly or quarterly projections for the first year. Then project from year to year.

Include a ratio and trend analysis for all of your financial statements. Use colorful graphs to explain positive trends, as part of the financial projections section of your business plan.

How to Write a Business Plan

Appendix

The appendix should not be part of the main body of your business plan. It should only be provided on a need to know basis. Your business plan may be seen by a lot of people and you don't want certain information available to everybody. Lenders may need such information so you should have an appendix ready just in case.

The appendix would include:

Credit history (personal & business)

- Resumes of key managers
- Product pictures
- Letters of reference
- Details of market studies
- Relevant magazine articles or book references
- Licenses, permits or patents
- Legal documents
- Copies of leases

How to Write a Business Plan

Building permits

Contracts

List of business consultants, including attorney and accountant

Keep a record of who you allow to see your business plan.

Include a Private Placement Disclaimer. A Private Placement Disclaimers is a private placement memorandum (PPM) is a document focused mainly on the possible downsides of an investment.

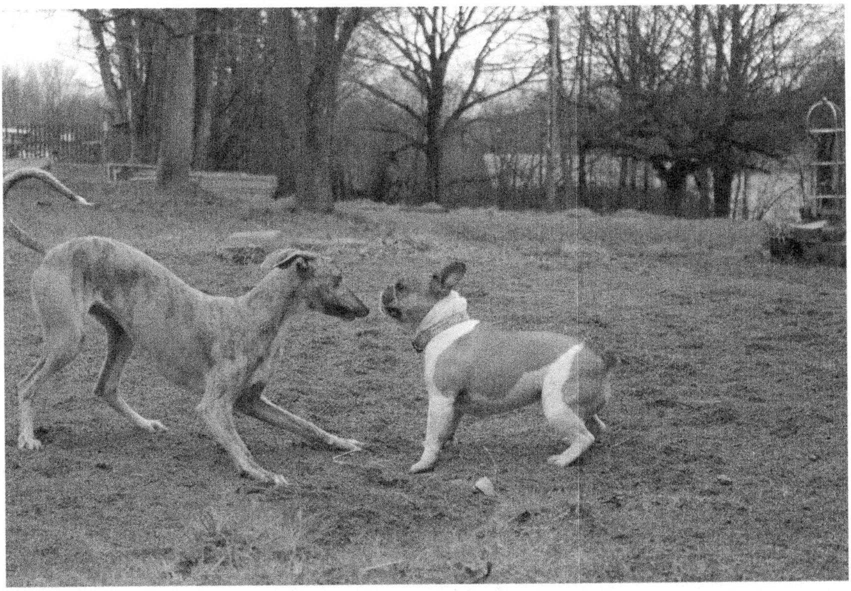

Chapter 4

Business Funding

Crowd Funding Crowd Sourcing

In 2015 over $34 billion dollars was raised by crowdfunding. Crowdfunding and Crowdsourcing roots began in 2005 and they help to finance or fund projects by raising money from a large number of people, usually by using the internet.

This type of fundraising or venture capital usually has 3 components. The individual or organization with a project that needs funding, groups of people who donate to the project, and a organization sets up a structure or rules to put the tow together.

These websites do charge fees. The standard fee for success is about %5. If your goal is not met there is also a fee.

Below is a list of the top Crowdfunding websites according to myself and Entrepreneur Magazine Contributor Sally Outlaw.

Crowd Funding Crowd Sourcing

https://www.crowdrise.com/

The leading online fundraising platform for nonprofits, companies, and events.

https://www.realtymogul.com/

"Commercial Real Estate Investing for Discerning investors" RealtyMogul.com launched in 2013 their mission: simplify real estate investing by connecting investors through cutting-edge technology.

https://www.gofundme.com/

This fundraising website allows for business, charity, education, emergencies, sports, medical, memorials, animals, faith, family, newlyweds etc...

https://www.youcaring.com/

The leader in free fundraising. Over $400 million raised.

Crowd Funding Crowd Sourcing

https://fundrazr.com/

"FundRazr is laser-focused on eliminating the guesswork of raising money online for your campaign. Our technology and social media guidance make telling your powerful story easy; sharing it with the widest community simple; and collecting the money worry-free. "

https://www.indiegogo.com/

Started as a platform for getting movies made, now helps to raise funds any cause.

http://rockethub.com/

Started as a platform for the arts, now it helps to raise funds for business, science, social projects and education.

http://peerbackers.com/

Peerbackers focuses on raising funds for business, entrepreneurs and innovators.

Crowd Funding Crowd Sourcing

http://group.growvc.com/

This website is for business and technology innovation.

https://microventures.com/

Get access to angel investors. This website is for business startups.

https://angel.co/

Another website for business startups.

https://circleup.com/

Circle up is for innovative consumer companies.

https://www.patreon.com/

If you start a YouTube Channel (highly recommended) you will hear about this website frequently. This website if for creative content people.

Crowd Funding Crowd Sourcing

https://www.kickstarter.com/

The most popular and well known of all the crowdfunding websites. Kickstarter focuses on film, music, technology, gaming, design and the creative arts. Kickstarter only accepts projects from the United States, Canada and the United Kingdom.

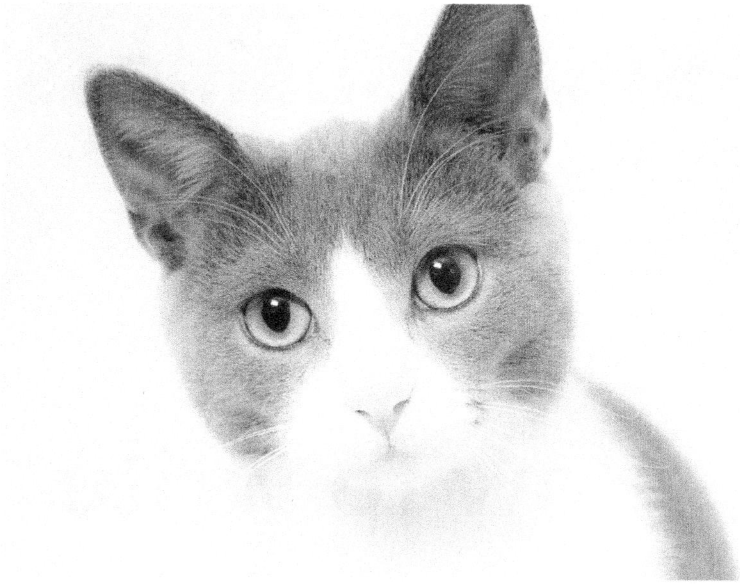

Chapter 5

Small Business Grants

How to write a Winning Grant Proposal

Small Business Grants

Government grants. Many people either don't believe government grants exist or they don't think they would ever be able to get government grant money.

First lets make one thing clear. Government grant money is **YOUR MONEY**. Government money comes from taxes paid by residents of this country. Depending on what state you live in, you are paying taxes on almost everything....Property tax for your house. Property tax on your car. Taxes on the things you purchase in the mall, or at the gas station. Taxes on your gasoline, taxes the food you buy etc.

So get yourself in the frame of mind that you are not a charity case or too proud to ask for help, because billionaire companies like GM, Big Banks and most of Corporate America is not hesitating to get their share of **YOUR MONEY**!

There are over two thousand three hundred (2,300) Federal Government Assistance Programs. Some are loans but many are formula grants and project grants. To see all of the programs available go to:

http://www.CFDA.gov

Small Business Grants

https://www.sbir.gov/

SBIR

The Small Business Innovation Research (SBIR) program is a program that has a lot of competition.

It encourages small businesses that exist inside the United States, to participate in Federal Research/Research and Development (R/R&D) that has the potential for financial gain.

Through a competitive awards-based program, Small Business Innovation Research program gives small businesses the opportunity to search for and reach their technological potential and provides the incentive to profit from its application to business.

By including qualified small businesses in the nation"s R&D arena, we encourage interest in high-tech innovation and the country gains the entrepreneurial spirit as it meets its specific research and development needs.

Small Business Grants

WRITING A GRANT PROPOSAL

The Basic Components of a Proposal

There are eight basic components to creating a solid proposal package:

1. The proposal summary;
2. Introduction of organization;
3. The problem statement   (or needs assessment);
4. Project objectives;
5. Project methods or design;
6. Project evaluation;
7. Future funding; and
8. The project budget.

Small Business Grants

The Proposal Summary

The Proposal Summary is an outline of the project goals and objectives. Keep the Proposal Summary short and to the point. No more than 2 or 3 paragraphs. Put it at the beginning the proposal.

Introduction

The Introduction portion of your grant proposal presents you and your business as a credible applicant and organization.

Highlight the accomplishments of your organization from all sources: newspaper or online articles etc. Include a biography of key members and leaders. State the goals and philosophy of the company.

The Problem Statement

The problem statement makes clear the problem you are going to solve(maybe reduce homelessness). Make sure to use facts. State who and how those affected will benefits from solving the problem. State the exact manner in how you will solve the problem.

Small Business Grants

Project Objectives

The Project Objectives section of your grant proposal focuses on the Goals and Desired outcome.

Make sure to indentify all objectives and how you are going to reach these objectives. The more statistics you can find to support your objectives the better. Make sure to put in realistic objectives. You may be judged on how well you accomplish what you said you intended to do.

Program Methods and Design

The program methods and design section of your grant proposal is a detailed plan of action.

>What resources are going to be used.

>What staff is going to be needed.

>System development

>Create a Flow Chart of project features.

>Explain what will be achieved.

>Try to produce evidence of what will be achieved.

>Make a diagram of program design.

Small Business Grants

Evaluation

There is product evaluation and process evaluation. The product evaluation deals with the result that relate to the project and how well the project has met it's objectives.

The process evaluation deals with how the project was conducted, how did it line up the original stated plan and the overall effectiveness of the different aspects of the plan.

Evaluations can start at anytime during the project or at the project's conclusion. It is advised to submit a evaluation design at the start of a project.

It looks better if you have collected convincing data before and during the program.

If evaluation design is not presented at the beginning that might encourage a critical review of the program design.

Future Funding

The Future Funding part of the grant proposal should have long term project planning past the grant period.

Small Business Grants

Budget

Utilities, rental equipment, staffing, salary, food, transportation, phone bills and insurance are just some of the things to include in the budget.

A well constructed budget accounts for every penny.

A complete guide for government grants is available at the website link below.

https://www.cfda.gov/downloads/CFDA.GOV_Public_User_Guide_v2.0.pdf

The guide can also be accessed at the very bottom of every page of the https://www.cfda.gov/ website.

Small Business Grants

Other sources of Government Funding

Get $500 to 5.5 Million to fund your business!

There are loans guaranteed by the Small Business Administration that range from $500 to $5,000,000 and can be used for almost any business purpose. Long-term fixed assets and operating capital. Some loan programs do have restrictions on how you can use the funds, so see a SBA-approved lender when you are requesting a loan. The lender can match you with the correct loan for your business needs.

To get General Small Business loans from the government. Go to the Small Business Administration for more information.

https://www.sba.gov/funding-programs/loans

SBA Microloan Program

The Microloan program provides loans of up to $50,000 with the average loan being $13,000.

https://www.sba.gov/

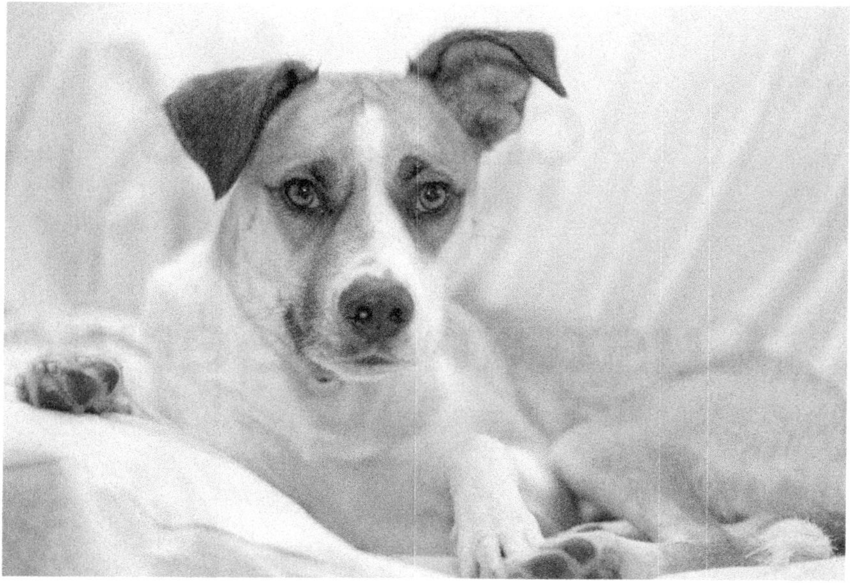

Chapter 6

Customer Service

Customer Service

Amazon is the #1 online retailer in the world. If a customer has a complaint it can go all the way to the top, Jeff Bezos. Jeff Bezos is the founder of Amazon. From watching the biography of Jeff Bezos. I got the distinct impression that none of the managers were going to let that happen. One of the reasons Amazon is the number one online retailer, is their customer service. "Customers want low prices and huge selection. Those things will never change." Jeff Bezos. He also believes in shipping fast and taking care of complaints quickly.

Walt Disney World is the number 1 theme park and vacation destination in the world. They call it the "happiess place on earth for a reason". Their customer service is second to none. Almost all employees are friendly, profesional and helpful.

Too many companies and businesses do not put enough thought into customer service. Have you ever walked into an auto parts store....stood there with your money and a product you wanted to purchase, in your hand and had to wait for the employee to get off the phone with a tire kicker, a possible customer? I have literally walked out the store and paid more money somewhere else then stand there and wait for somebody who called the auto part store because they needed someone to talk to.

Customer Service

Here are a few customer service tips for business.

1. Be friendly and use the greeting of the day.

2. Remain calm when dealing with a hot head.

3. Be professional when dealing with refund requests. A good rule of thumb is to budget %10 of your gross for refunds.

4. Respond to phone calls and emails as quickly as possible.

5. Have knowledgable people answering the phone or dealing with the public.

Customer Service

6. If shipping a product. Ship it fast or give the customer a reason for the delay and let them decide if they still want the product.

7. Don't take customer insults personal. Some people are just mad at the world.

8. Conversly don't allow your employees or yourself to be abused. As Ron Legrand once said "Sometimes you have to fire the customer."

9. Try to deliver more than promised.

10. Prioritize. The customer standing in front of you waiting to pay is more important than the one thinking about buying.

Customer Service

A recent survey revealed the top rated customer service companies. Here is a list of the top 24 customer service companies in the world. What do they do, that you can add to your customer service mission statement?

1. Amazon

2. Marriot Hotels

3. Hilton Hotels

4. UPS United Parcel Service

5. Fedex Federal Express

6. Google

7. State Farm Insurance

Customer Service

8. Samsung

9. Trader Joe's

10. Lowe's

11. Sony

12. Publix Groceries

13. Southwest Airlines

14. Kroger Groceries

15. Subway Sandwiches

Customer Service

16. Petsmart

17. Apple Inc

18. Costco Wholesale

19. Home Depot

20. Yahoo!

21. Netflix

22. American Express

23. Barnes & Noble

24. MicroSoft

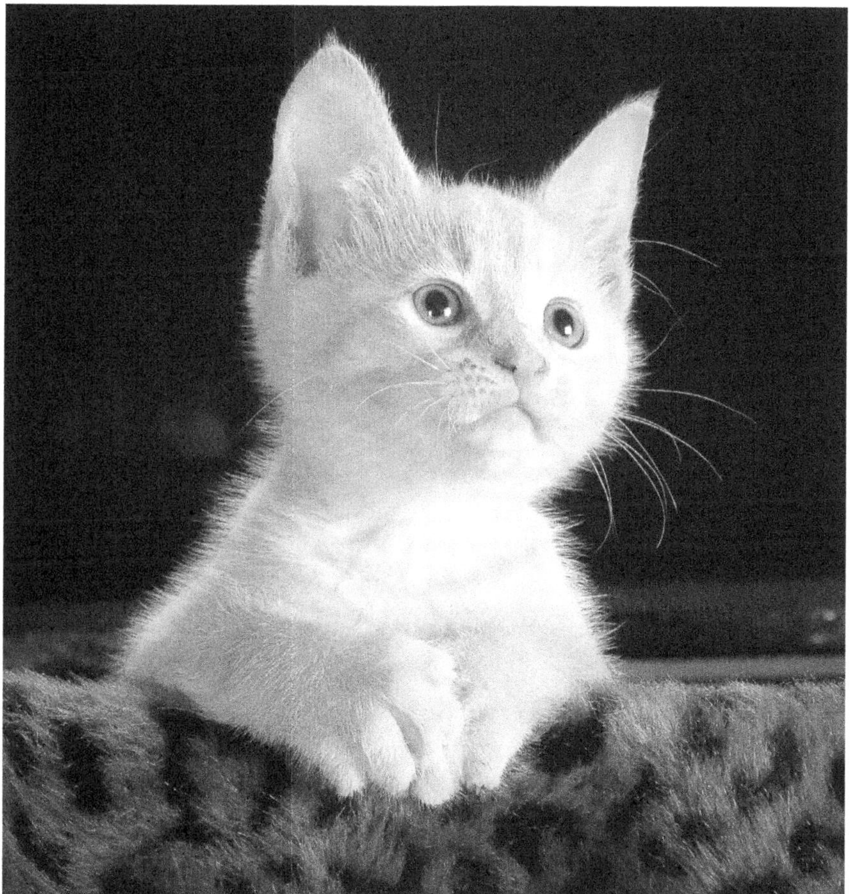

Chapter 7

Zero Cost Marketing

Pet Sitter Marketing

Website

Today marketing a business begins with getting a website. Below are some top web hosting companies. All of these hosting companies fees start at less than $5.00 a month.

1. Bluehost.com

2. ipage.com

3. Hostgator.com

4. sitebuilder.com

5. justhost.com

6. fatcow.com

7. domain.com

8. starlogic.com

9. Yahoo.com

10. godaddy.com

Pet Sitter Marketing

YouTube

Once your website is up, you have to send traffic to it. One way is to create YouTube videos. We have a complete set of YouTube & Email Marketing training videos to teach you step by step how to reach thousands of clients with of free advertising. Available at the link below.

https://goo.gl/nLXDqb

If you don't have one, open up a YouTube account and channel at www.YouTube.com.

You can use a phone, camera or screen capture software to make your videos.

Create and upload your videos.

Posting videos on YouTube is a free and very effective way to market you business. Study other successful videos on YouTube to get an idea of how to create successful videos. Below are some examples of good Pet Sitting promotion videos.

10 Must Know Tips for Pet Sitters

https://goo.gl/iqfDC1

Pet Sitter Marketing

YouTube

Knock Your Pet Sitting Clients Socks Off The First 100 Days!

https://goo.gl/WR5JkJ

Study the headlines, the content and the format for ideas for your own videos.

You can hire out people to make your videos for less than 20 dollars. Simply go to www.fiverr.com and type in "make youtube video".

Pet Sitter Marketing

YouTube

"It's not about you." ...The Ancient One

Marvel's Dr. Strange.

When I first started trying to make money on YouTube, my main goal was just that. To make money for me. It took a while for me to learn that the videos that had the best traffic and got shared on social media, where the videos, that were "not about me." In other words, they had little promotion and just gave solid researched valuable information for free.

You can use these top business websites as information to help your YouTube viewers and thus help increase the amount of times your video gets shared, liked, and commented on. Even if you do not sell the type of products or information contained in the video, you can increase your brand as an expert in the field. Or you can see if these businesses offer affiliate programs and get a portion of a sale, by placing a link in the description of the video.

You can also use these websites for research to see what makes these websites some of the best in the business and what you can add to your business to duplicate their success.

Pet Sitter Marketing

YouTube

www.jackiescaninecompanioncare.com

www.shannonspetsitting.net

www.thewoofpack.com

www.petsittingdirectory.com

www.daisys-petsitting.com

www.arizonapetsitting.com

www.thepetnanny.net

www.petandhousesittingbellevuewa.com

Pet Sitter Marketing

YouTube

www.petpals.com

www.petsitting1.com

www.profpetsit.com

www.sweetiescathouse.com

www.crittercaretakers.com

www.petsitting.com

www.crittersitterswi.com

www.leashesandlitterboxesatlanta.com

Pet Sitter Marketing

YouTube

www.petsitter.com

www.txpetsitters.com

www.trophyclubpetpro.com

www.spartapetsitters.com

Pet Sitter Marketing

Rover.com

Rover.com is a website service that started in June of 2011 that offers these services...

* Dog Boarding

* House Sitting

* Drop In visits

* Doggy Day Care

* Dog Walking

The company serves as a go between pet client and pet service and makes approximately %15 - %40 commission on jobs arranged from their website.

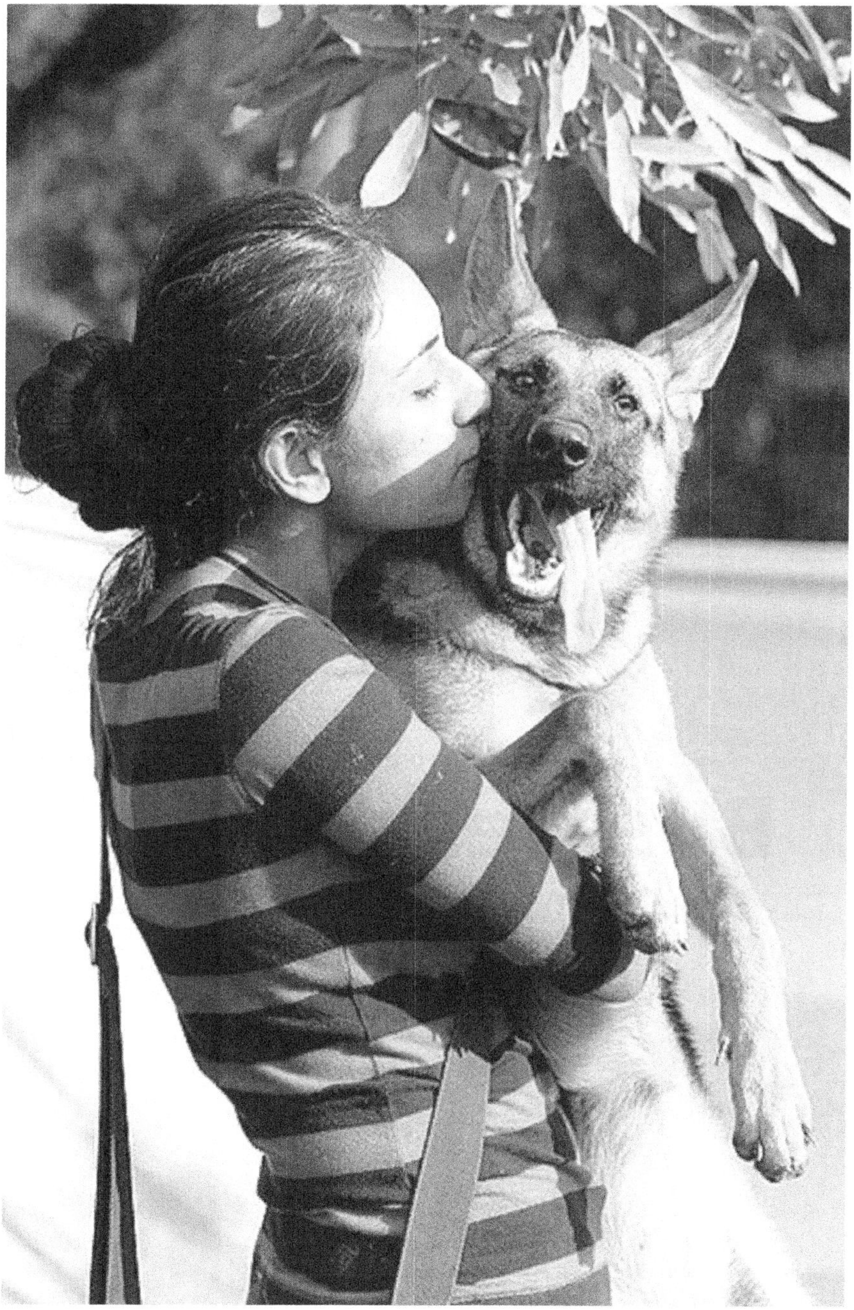

Chapter 8

Wholesale

Business Supplies

Pet Sitting Supplies

Pet Sitting Software
(free)

Pet sitting software can help you to manage a small or a growing business. There are free and paid version. Here is a list of free version of pet sitting software.

Pet Sitter (free to try)

Pet Sitter is an easy-to-use powerful tool, perfect for those who run pet-sitting or dog-walking business and for those who simply want to take care of their animal companions properly.

https://goo.gl/nujgJd

Power Pet Sitter for iPhone (free)

The Power Pet Sitter mobile application is designed to allow pet sitters the ability to view and complete their appointments quickly and easily.

https://goo.gl/iVaHCf

Pet Sitting Supplies

Pet Sitting Software
(Paid)

Time to Pet

You can customize what information you collect about your clients and their pets, accept credit/debit or ACH payments and even share GPS and timestamp data with your customers. All data is also protected using the same 128 bit level encryption your bank uses.

https://www.timetopet.com/

Pet Sit Click

PetSitClick not only includes standard features like customer tracking, scheduling, and accounting, but also industry leading features such as a drag and drop calendar, mapping tools, and mobile access.

https://www.petsitclick.com/

Pet Sitting Supplies

CERTIFICATION PROGRAMS

CCPDT

Certification Council for Professional Dog Trainers.

CCPDT started in November 1999 . The Association of Professional Dog Trainers (APDT) decided to create a certification program for dog trainers.

The CCPDT offers ....

* Dog Trainer Certification

* Behavior Consultant Certification

* Marketing Your Certification

* Continuing Education

* Recertification

* Dog Pro Profiles

http://www.ccpdt.org/

The Association of Professional Dog Trainers (ADPT)

https://apdt.com/

Pet Sitting Supplies

Pet Wholesaler

PetWholesaler.com, is an online B2B (Business to Business) Web portal for Pet Retailers to purchase wholesale pet supplies. Petwholesaler offers supplies for Dogs, Cats, Birds, Reptiles, Horses, Aquarium, Small Animals, Exotic Animals etc from hundreds of manufacturers and distributors at greatly discounted prices.

http://www.petwholesaler.com/index.php

Pet Manufactuers

Wholesale pet products and supplies. Its vast array of online pet supplies, pet products and pet food applies to the wholesaler and online avid shopper too. Explore rows upon rows of pet-related items like pet clothing and pet accessories.

http://www.petmanufacturers.com/

King Wholesale

Offers free shipping, free catalogs and a variety of pet supllies.

http://www.kingwholesale.com/

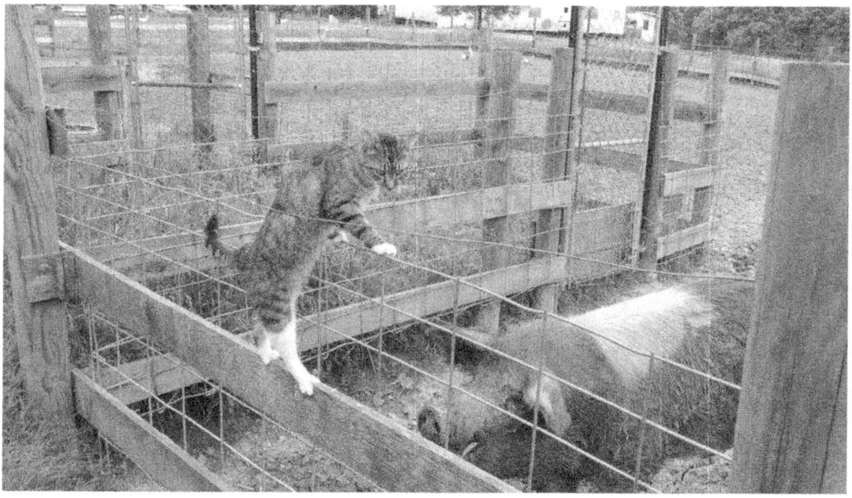

Chapter 9

Business Rolodex

Pet Sitter Business Rolodex

Pet Sitting Insurance

http://petsits.com/articles/pet-sitting-insurance-providers

http://psi.petsitterinsurance.com/

http://petsits.com/insurance.htm

https://www.petcareins.com/

Pet Sitting Certification

http://petsitters.org

http://www.petsitters.org/napps_certification.php

https://www.petsit.com/certificate

Pet Sitter Business Rolodex

Pet Sitting Software

(free) http://download.cnet.com/s/pet-sitter/

https://www.timetopet.com/

https://www.petsitclick.com/

http://download.cnet.com/Pet-Sitter/3000-2064_4-10901631.html

Dog & Cat Organizations

http://www.acfacat.com/

http://www.adbadogs.com/p_home.asp

http://www.arba.org/

http://www.iwdba.org/

Pet Sitter Business Rolodex

Training Supplies

http://www.petwholesaler.com/index.php

http://www.petmanufacturers.com/

http://www.futurepet.com/

http://www.kingwholesale.com/

http://petsmart.com

http://petco.com

http://www.dog-training.com/

http://www.roverpet.com/

http://www.dogsupplies.com/

http://www.happytailsspa.com/

http://www.k9bytesgifts.com/

http://www.upco.com/

Pet Sitter Business Rolodex

List of recognized Cat & Dog Breeds

http://cattime.com/cat-breeds

http://www.akc.org/dog-breeds/

CERTIFICATION PROGRAMS

http://www.ccpdt.org/

https://apdt.com/join/certification/

Dog Information

www.rainbowridgekennels.com

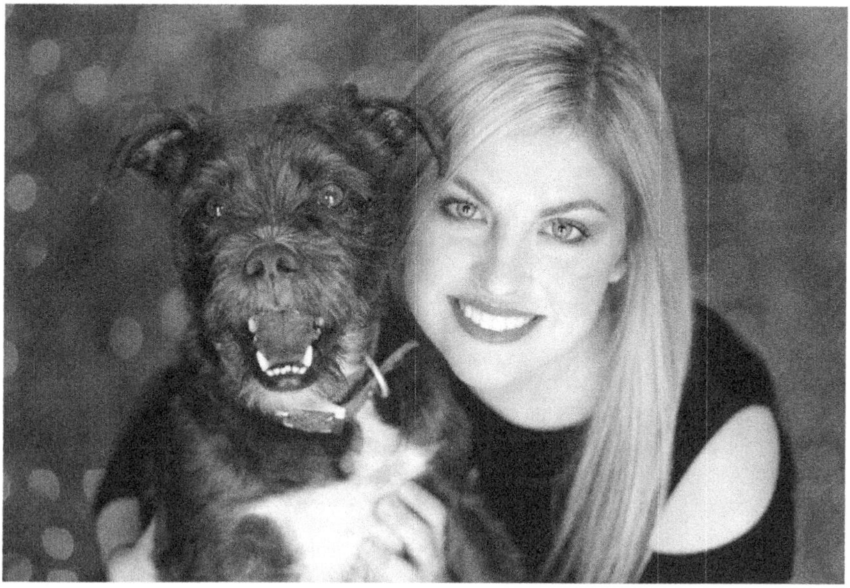

Chapter 10

Business Terms

Business Terms & Definitions

Accounts – Companies produce a annual set of accounts. If you are listed on the stock exchange you have to give info on profits six months into the financial year.

Actuary – Actuaries work for insurance companies and pension providers and calculate life expectancy, accident rates and likely payouts by using math algorithms.

Business Plan - A **business plan** is a formal statement of business goals, reasons they are attainable, and plans for reaching them. It may also contain background information about the organization or team attempting to reach those goals.

Balance Sheet - a statement of the assets, liabilities, and capital of a business or other organization at a particular point in time, detailing the balance of income and expenditure over the preceding period.

Business Terms & Definitions

Bear Market - A stock market in which share prices fall precipitously, typically 15%-20%.

Bull Market - A market when prices roar ahead.

Capital Gains - A **capital gain** refers to profit that results from a sale of a capital asset, such as stock, bond or real estate, where the sale price exceeds the purchase price. The gain is the difference between a higher selling price and a lower purchase price

Capital Gains Tax - a tax levied on profit from the sale of property or of an investment.

Chapter 11 Bankruptcy - Chapter 11 is a chapter of Title 11 of the United States Bankruptcy Code, which permits reorganization under the bankruptcy laws of the United States. Chapter 11 bankruptcy is available to every business, whether organized as a corporation, partnership or sole proprietorship, and to individuals, although it is most prominently used by corporate entities

Business Terms & Definitions

Consumers Prices Index - The **Consumer Price Index** (CPI) is a measure that examines the weighted average of **prices** of a basket of **consumer** goods and services, such as transportation, food and medical care. It is calculated by taking **price** changes for each item in the predetermined basket of goods and averaging them.

Day Trading (g) - Day trading is the buying and selling of stocks during the trading day by punters on their own account.
The aim is to make a profit on the day and have no open positions at the close of the trading session.

Dow Jones Industrial Average (i) - The **Dow Jones Industrial Average** (**DJIA**) is a price-weighted **average** of 30 significant stocks traded on the New York Stock Exchange (NYSE) and the NASDAQ. The **DJIA** was invented by Charles **Dow** back in 1896.

Diminishing Returns (I) - used to refer to a point at which the level of profits or benefits gained is less than the amount of money or energy invested.

Business Terms & Definitions

Economic Growth - Economic growth is the increase in the inflation-adjusted market value of the goods and services produced by an economy over time. It is conventionally measured as the percent rate of increase in real gross domestic product or real GDP.

Equity - the value of the shares issued by a company.

Elasticity - Elasticity is a measure of a variable's sensitivity to a change in another variable. In business and economics, **elasticity** refers the degree to which individuals, consumers or producers change their demand or the amount supplied in response to price or income changes.

Fiscal Year - The US fiscal year runs from October 1 to September 30.

Foreign Exchange (Forex) - Foreign exchange, or forex, markets are where one currency is exchanged for another.

Business Terms & Definitions

FORM 501 - A 501(c) organization is a nonprofit organization in the federal law of the United States according to 26 U.S.C. § 501 and is one of 29 types of nonprofit organizations which are exempt from some federal income taxes.

Form 701 - General Information. Registration of a Limited Liability Partnership.

Grant - Grants are non-repayable **funds** or products disbursed or gifted by one party (**grant** makers), often a government department, corporation, foundation or trust, to a recipient, often (but not always) a nonprofit entity, educational institution, business or an individual.

Gross Domestic Product - GDP is the sum of all goods and services produced in the economy, including the service sector, manufacturing, construction, energy, agriculture and government.

Business Terms & Definitions

Gross National Product - the total value of goods produced and services provided by a country during one year, equal to the gross domestic product plus the net income from foreign investments.

Hedge Funds - a limited partnership of investors that uses high risk methods, such as investing with borrowed money, in hopes of realizing large capital gains.

Income Statement - An **income statement** is one of the financial statements of a company and shows the company's revenues and expenses during a particular period.

Income Tax - tax levied by a government directly on income, especially an annual tax on personal income.

Inheritance Tax - a tax imposed on someone who inherits property or money.

Business Terms & Definitions

Inflation - a general increase in prices and fall in the purchasing value of money.

Limited liability company (LLC) - A limited liability company (LLC) is a corporate structure whereby the members of the company cannot be held personally liable for the company's debts or liabilities. Limited liability companies are essentially hybrid entities that combine the characteristics of a corporation and a partnership or sole proprietorship.

Loan to Value - The loan-to-value (LTV) ratio is a financial term used by lenders to express the ratio of a loan to the value of an asset purchased. The term is commonly used by banks and building societies to represent the ratio of the first mortgage line as a percentage of the total appraised value of real property.

Microloan - a small sum of money lent at low interest to a new business.

Business Terms & Definitions

Mutual Fund - an investment program funded by shareholders that trades in diversified holdings and is professionally managed.

Nasdaq - The National Association of Securities Dealers Automated Quotations (Nasdaq) was set up in 1971 as an international screen-based trading system without a central dealing floor. In 1998 it merged with the American Stock Exchange (Amex).

Occupational Pension Scheme - Occupational pension schemes may be contributory or non-contributory, funded or unfunded, defined benefit or defined contribution. In contributory schemes, both you and your employer pay contributions towards the scheme. In non-contributory schemes, you do not contribute but your employer does.

Partnership - A legal form of business operation between two or more individuals who share management and profits. The federal government recognizes several types of partnerships. The two most common are general and limited partnerships. . ... A limited partnership has both general and limited partners.

Business Terms & Definitions

Rate of Return - A **rate of return** is the gain or loss on an investment over a specified time period, expressed as a percentage of the investment's cost. Gains on investments are defined as income received plus any capital gains realized on the sale of the investment.

Real Estate Investment Trusts - A **real estate investment trust** (**REIT**) is a company that owns, and in most cases operates, income-producing real estate. REITs own many types of commercial real estate, ranging from office and apartment buildings to warehouses, shopping centers and hotels.

SBA - The **Small Business Administration** (**SBA**) is a U.S. government agency, formulated in 1953, that operates autonomously. This agency was established to bolster and promote the economy in general by providing assistance to small businesses.

Business Terms & Definitions

SCORE (SBA) - SCORE is a nonprofit organization that provides free business mentoring services to prospective and established small business owners in the United States. More than 10,000 volunteers provide these services, with all volunteers being active and retired business executives and entrepreneurs.

Sole proprietorship - A business that legally has no separate existence from its owner. Income and losses are taxed on the individual's personal income tax return. . The sole proprietorship is the simplest business form under which one can operate a business. The sole proprietorship is not a legal entity.

Tax Haven - Generic term for a geographical area outside the jurisdiction of one's home country which imposes only a few restrictions on legitimate **business**-activities within its jurisdiction, and little or no income **tax**. ... Also called low **tax** jurisdiction, non **tax** jurisdiction, or offshore **haven**.

Business Terms & Definitions

Value Added Tax - A value added tax (VAT) is a consumption tax added to a product's sales price. It represents a tax on the "value added" to the product throughout its production process.

Wall Street - Wall Street is a street in lower Manhattan that is the original home of the New York Stock Exchange and the historic headquarters of the largest U.S. brokerages and investment banks.

Yield - The yield is the income return on an investment, such as the interest or dividends received from holding a particular security. The yield is usually expressed as an annual percentage rate based on the investment's cost, current market value or face value.

Zero Interest Rates - A zero interest rate policy is a route taken by a central bank to keep the base rate at zero per cent in an attempt to stimulate demand in the economy by making the supply of money cheaper.

Thank you for Leaving a Book Review

You are such a nice person!!!

I have purchased all of the top real estate investing books on the market, and most have a handful of out dated web sites for their sources of properties.

There is not another real estate investing book on the market that gives you as many sources for wholesale real estate than this book.

This book also gives you a web site that has over 4,000 sources of real estate financing! Wow!

My book gives you more and in most cases for less!

I have enjoyed doing all the research and sharing my real world real estate investing experience in easy to understand dialog.

So please leave a great review!

Thank you. Warm Regards,

Brian Mahoney

Get Our Massive Money Complete Internet Marketing Video Training Program at:

(Zero Cost Internet Marketing complete 142 video series)

$1,997 Megasized Money Making Marketing Program

ONLY $67 !!!!

https://goo.gl/Qed1dY

Join Our VIP Mailing List and Get FREE Money Making Training Videos! Then Start Making Money within 24 hours!
Plus if you join our Mailing list you can get Revised and New Edition versions of your book free!

And Notifications of other FREE Offers!

Just Hit/Type in the Link Below

https://mahoneyproducts.wixsite.com/win1

Made in the USA
Coppell, TX
13 February 2023